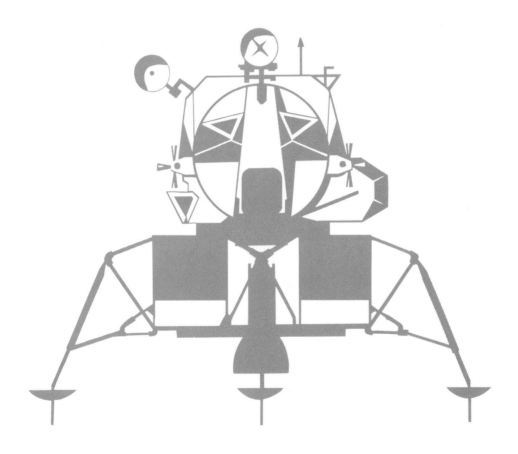

Writer: Robin Kerrod
Designer: Tri-Art
Illustrators: Jeff Burn, Roger Full Associates,
Tony Gibbons, John Harwood, John Kelly
Cover Illustrator: Jack Keay
Series Editor: Christopher Tunney
Art Director: Keith Groom

LIBRARY OF CONGRESS CATALOGING IN PUBLICATION DATA

Kerrod, Robin.
Race for the moon.

(The Question and answer books)
Includes index.
SUMMARY: Presents questions and answers about the moon
and space missions to the moon. Includes an appendix of U. S.
manned space flights.

1. Space flight to the moon—Juvenile literature. [1. Space
flight to the moon. 2. Questions and answers] I. Burn, Jeff.
II. Title.

TL799.M6K46   629.45'4   79-2347
ISBN 0-8225-1183-5   lib. bdg.

This revised edition © 1980 by Lerner Publications Company.
First edition copyright © 1978 by Sackett Publicare Ltd.

International Standard Book Number: 0-8225-1183-5
Library of Congress Catalog Card Number: 79-2347

Manufactured in the United States of America

2   3   4   5   6   7   8   9   10   85   84   83

The Question and Answer Books

RACE FOR THE
Moon

4 Our Neighbor the Moon
6 Moon Myths
8 Reaching for the Moon (1)
10 Reaching for the Moon (2)
12 Before Apollo
14 Project Apollo (1)
16 Project Apollo (2)
18 Destination Moon (1)
20 Destination Moon (2)
22 The Moon-Walkers
24 Lunarnauts at Work
26 Homeward Bound
28 After Apollo
30 Moon Base
32 U.S. Manned Spaceflights
34 Landing on Another World
35 Index

Lerner Publications Company ▪ Minneapolis

Can we tell what the Moon is like from Earth?

We can see the Moon quite clearly through powerful telescopes and can distinguish its main surface features. They are the rugged highlands, which are light in color, and vast, low-lying maria ("seas"), which are dark. Everywhere craters can be seen, especially in the highlands.

OUR NEIGHBOR THE MOON On October 4, 1957, a new moon appeared in the sky. It was the first artificial satellite, the Russian Sputnik 1. As first Russian and then American scientists put more spacecraft into orbit, their eyes turned to a new target. It was the Moon, our natural satellite, some 240,000 miles (385,000 km) away in space. Soon a race appeared to be developing between the two powers to send men to the Moon. Who would get there first?

Sea of Serenity

Sea of Crises

Sea of Showers

Sea of Vapors

Sea of Tranquility

Ocean of Storms

Sea of Clouds

Sea of Fertility

Sea of Nectar

Sea of Moisture

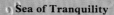

How do spacecraft help in studying the Moon?

Spacecraft can approach much closer to the Moon and even land on it. They can photograph its surface in minute detail and spot things we cannot see from Earth. They can return to Earth with samples of Moon soil. They can view the far side of the Moon, which we can never see from Earth.

Do we know where the Moon came from?

Pacific Ocean

Earth

Moon

There are several different ideas about how the Moon came into being. For a long time people thought that it was torn from the Earth, from the region that is now the Pacific Ocean. But scientists think this is most unlikely. They think that the Moon probably formed as a separate body at the same time as the Earth.

Why should humans go to the Moon?

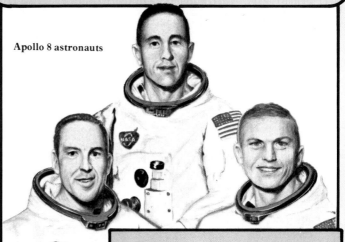

Apollo 8 astronauts

People can do many more things than a spacecraft can. They are much better observers, and can think and act independently. They can roam much farther afield and examine and photograph anything that seems interesting.

Man in the Moon

In fairy stories and nursery rhymes, we often read about or see pictures of "the man in the Moon." The reason is obvious if you look at the crescent Moon. The dark mare (sea) known as the Sea of Crises looks like an eye, and the other dark maria look like a cheek and a mouth.

MOON MYTHS The Moon has fascinated people from the earliest times. They were grateful for its pale light, which helped to reduce the dangers of the night. They marveled at the way it changed its shape from day to day, and they eventually used these changes (its phases) to make up a calendar. The Moon came to play an important part in people's lives. They began to make up stories about the Moon and its mysterious powers, and dream of traveling there.

The Moon and Luck

Because of its pale silvery light, the Moon became associated with the idea of riches —for silver is a precious metal. Many coins used to be made of silver, and it was said that you would have good fortune if you turned silver coins in your pocket when looking at the new Moon.

Werewolves and Lunacy

A more widely held belief was that the light from the full Moon could affect the mind. Madness could result. Another word for madness—lunacy—comes from the Latin word for Moon. From eastern Europe came tales of how men changed into wolves ("werewolves") at the time of the full Moon. There is no truth in either of these ideas.

Diana the Moon Goddess

Most of the early civilizations worshipped the Moon, which was thought to possess strange powers. The Romans called their Moon goddess Diana. She was one of the most important deities and was also goddess of the hunt. The crescent Moon was her bow, and moonbeams were her arrows.

The Moon and Weather

Many country folk believe that you can foretell the weather from the appearance of the Moon. A halo around the Moon and "the Moon on its back" are signs of bad weather. They also say that the phases of the Moon affect the weather.

In Literature

French writer Cyrano de Bergerac (1619–1655), famed for the length of his nose, was one of the earliest science fiction writers. In one story he tells how he was propelled to the Moon by firecrackers.

The French novelist Jules Verne (1828–1905) wrote stirring tales of trips to the Moon in *From the Earth to the Moon* and *Round the Moon*. Their heroes were launched to the Moon by cannon.

A little later in England, H. G. Wells (1866–1946) "sent" two men to the Moon in his book *First Men in the Moon*. They went in a spacecraft which they propelled by manipulating the force of gravity.

Is it difficult to escape from Earth's pull?

REACHING FOR THE MOON (1) Sending spacecraft to the Moon requires a lot more power than putting a satellite into orbit. In orbit, a satellite is still firmly held in the grip of the Earth's gravity. It simply balances this gravity by virtue of its speed. To reach the Moon, a spacecraft has to escape from the Earth's gravity and let itself be drawn instead by the gravity of the Moon.

A spacecraft can escape from the powerful grip of gravity only if it is launched toward the sky at a very fast speed—about 25,000 mph (40,000 kph). This speed is known as the *escape velocity*.

Escape velocity 25,000 mph

Orbital velocity 17,000 mph

How do you aim at the Moon?

You cannot send a spacecraft to the Moon by aiming it right at the Moon. For one thing, a spacecraft always travels in a curve. And the Moon is a moving target. As a result, you have to aim the spacecraft so that it arrives at a point in space at the same time as the Moon.

Earth

Day 2

Day 2

Day 1

Day 1

Path of spacecraft

Moon traveling in orbit

What was the first spacecraft to:

Fly to the Moon?

Russian space scientists launched the first spacecraft to the Moon on January 2, 1959. Known as Luna, or Lunik, 1, the probe passed within 3,700 miles (6,000 km) of the Moon. It was the first spacecraft to achieve escape velocity.

Touch the Moon?

Luna 1 was a spherical craft carrying aerials and several instruments. It looked much like Luna 2, launched on September 12 of the same year. Luna 2 actually hit the Moon, not far from the crater Archimedes.

Photograph the far side?

Right on the heels of Luna 2, Luna 3 was launched on October 4. It was a much more advanced craft, equipped with solar cells and a camera. It sent back the first photographs of the Moon's far side.

What was the Ranger spacecraft like?

Early American attempts to reach the Moon were unsuccessful until July 1964, when a Ranger 7 spacecraft sent back high-quality pictures before it crashed on the Moon. The Ranger probes carried six television cameras and were powered by solar cells.

How can we soft-land a spacecraft on the Moon?

After the Luna and Ranger successes in hitting the Moon, space scientists began designing probes that would land gently on the Moon. Soft-landing probes must have a rocket motor to slow them down before they reach the surface.

What spacecraft first soft-landed on the Moon?

The Russians were the first to soft-land a spacecraft on the Moon, in February 1966. It was in the form of an instrument capsule released by the main spacecraft, Luna 9. It sent back the first close-up pictures of the lunar landscape.

Can parachutes be used to slow a spacecraft down?

When spacecraft return to the Earth after a space flight, they use parachutes to help slow them down. This is possible because the Earth has air around it. The Moon has no air, so parachutes cannot be used. Firing retro-rockets toward the surface is the only way to brake probes for a soft-landing.

What did Surveyor tell us?

It could be argued that the Luna 9 landing was not a true soft-landing. But those of the later American Surveyor probes certainly were. From the way they landed, scientists knew that the lunar surface must be firm. The surface material seemed to be like fine soil on Earth.

Why were the Lunar Orbiters so important?

With each new lunar probe, scientists began to get a much clearer picture of what the Moon was like. Their next step was to put probes into lunar orbit. Most successful were the U.S. Lunar Orbiters, which mapped the whole surface in great detail, especially the proposed sites for the Apollo landings.

What was the Mercury spacecraft like?

BEFORE APOLLO On April 12, 1961, the Russians put the first man into orbit—Yuri Gagarin. Within a month the American president, John F. Kennedy, firmly committed the American people to a manned Moon landing "by 1970." The first American in orbit was John H. Glenn, on February 20, 1962, flying in a Mercury spacecraft. Other Mercury and later Gemini flights paved the way for the ambitious Apollo Moon-landing project.

The Mercury spacecraft was designed to carry a single astronaut. It was only about 11.5 feet (3.5 meters) long and 6.5 feet (2 meters) in diameter at its widest point. At launch it was topped by an escape tower which the astronaut could use in an emergency. There were six manned Mercury flights.

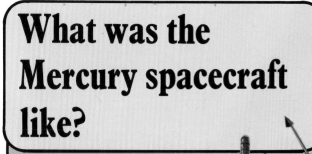

Launching tower

Escape tower

Retro-rockets

What is a sub-orbital flight?

The first two Mercury flights were sub-orbital—that is, the astronauts did not go into orbit. They were simply propelled in an arcing path which took them some 112 miles (180 km) high and 310 miles (500 km) from the launching site.

What was the Gemini spacecraft like?

Crew module

Equipment module

The Gemini was a much bigger, two-man craft, about 20 feet (6 m) long and 10 feet (3 m) across at its widest point. It consisted of two parts, or *modules*. One contained the crew, the other equipment and rocket motors. The first of nine Gemini flights took place on March 23, 1965.

Which spacecraft made the first rendezvous?

Gemini 7

The first space rendezvous between manned craft took place between Gemini 6 and Gemini 7 in December, 1965. The Gemini 6 astronauts maneuvered to within 6.5 feet (2 m) of the other craft, and the two flew in tight formation for several hours.

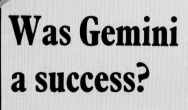

Gemini 6

Was Gemini a success?

Gemini was a spectacular success on all counts. By the end of the program, the United States had overtaken Russia in the number of man-hours spent in space.

How was Apollo able to reach the Moon and return?

PROJECT APOLLO (1) By the end of 1966 the Gemini astronauts had shown that it was possible to rendezvous and dock (link up) with other spacecraft and "walk" in space. In 1967 three astronauts were killed during training inside an Apollo spacecraft, and this caused delay while the craft was redesigned. The first manned Apollo flight took place in October, 1968, and two months later Apollo 8 made a triumphant circumnavigation of the Moon. The stage was set for the first Moon landing.

The method was known as "lunar orbiter rendezvous." It required one part, or module, of the spacecraft to descend to the Moon and then later rendezvous with the main craft.

What was the Command Module?

The Apollo spacecraft was made up of three modules in all. The three astronauts forming the crew were housed in very cramped conditions in what was called the Command Module. The module was pressurized and had a thick heat shield to protect the astronauts.

What was the Service Module?

The Service Module was attached to the base of the Command Module. It housed a powerful rocket motor and propellant tanks, together with fuel cells to make electricity, and other equipment.

What was the Lunar Module?

The Lunar Module was the part that descended to the Moon's surface with two astronauts inside. In the flight to the Moon it was attached to the Command Module, as shown in the picture on the right.

Ascent section

Descent section

How big were the modules?

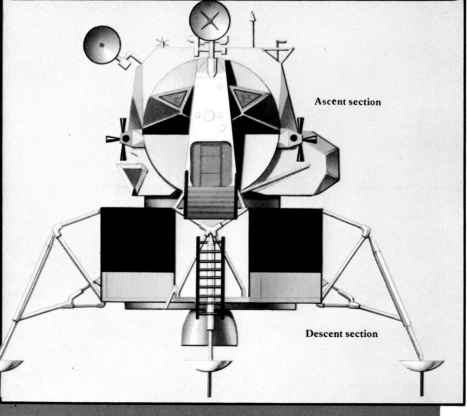

20 ft (6 m)

10 ft 6 in (3·2 m)

14 ft (4·3 m)

10 ft 6 in (3·2 m)

13 ft (3·9 m)

15

How was the Apollo spacecraft launched?

The Apollo spacecraft was one of the most complicated pieces of equipment ever assembled. Its three modules together weighed more than 40 tons. A very powerful rocket had to be designed to dispatch such a load to the Moon. It was the Saturn V, the biggest rocket ever built.

How big was it?

On the launch pad Saturn V stood a towering 364 feet (111 m) high from the end of the rocket nozzles to the tip of the escape tower. At its widest point it was 33 feet (10 m) across. Most of its bulk was taken up with propellants for the rockets.

Who designed Saturn V?

V-2 rocket

The Saturn V rocket was the brainchild of Wernher von Braun (1912–1977). Born in Germany, he directed the research team that developed the V-2 rocket. He went to the United States after World War II.

How many stages did Saturn have?

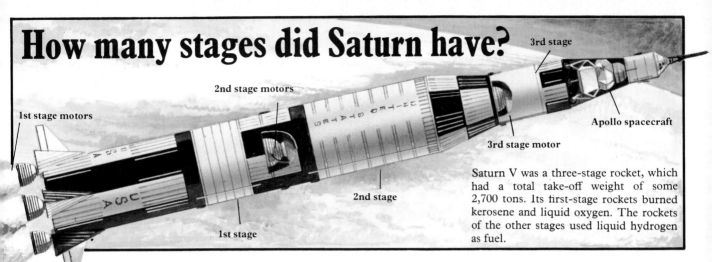

1st stage motors · 2nd stage motors · 3rd stage · Apollo spacecraft · 3rd stage motor · 2nd stage · 1st stage

Saturn V was a three-stage rocket, which had a total take-off weight of some 2,700 tons. Its first-stage rockets burned kerosene and liquid oxygen. The rockets of the other stages used liquid hydrogen as fuel.

Where was it assembled?

Assembly of Saturn V took place in the Vehicle Assembly Building at the Kennedy Space Center in Florida, 3 miles (5 km) from the launch pad. One of the biggest buildings in the world, it has a length of 715 feet (218 m), a width of 518 feet (158 m), and a height of 525 feet (160 m).

How was it moved to the launch pad?

Inside the Vehicle Assembly Building the Saturn rocket was assembled, with launch pad and tower, on top of the biggest vehicle in the world. This was a massive crawler transporter whose top speed was 0.4 mph (0.6 kph).

DESTINATION MOON (1) The preparations for the Apollo flights to the Moon were lengthy and painstaking. Nothing could be left to chance. The multitude of systems in the spacecraft and its launching rocket were checked and rechecked as the countdown began a few days before launching. Finally all was ready. The rocket motors were ignited, and the huge rocket climbed into the sky.

How long did it take Apollo to get into orbit?

From the moment of ignition of the first-stage engines, it took Saturn V only 12 minutes to boost Apollo into orbit. By this time it had dropped its first two stages and its third stage had shut off. Apollo was then traveling at 17,000 mph (28,000 kph).

Third stage shuts off
Spacecraft is in orbit
12 minutes after lift-off

Second stage separates
Third stage fires
9 minutes after lift-off

Escape tower separates

First stage separates
Second stage fires
2½ minutes after lift-off

Lift-off

Why did it go into a parking orbit?

Apollo was put into a so-called parking orbit—rather than sent directly to the Moon—for safety's sake. While in orbit, the astronauts checked out all spacecraft systems to make sure they worked perfectly. Only then did they head for the Moon.

What maneuvers did the astronauts have to make?

After firing the third-stage motor to boost them toward the Moon, the astronauts had to maneuver their craft into the correct flight position. The Apollo Command Module had to do an about-turn and link with the Lunar Module, before pulling it clear of the unwanted third stage.

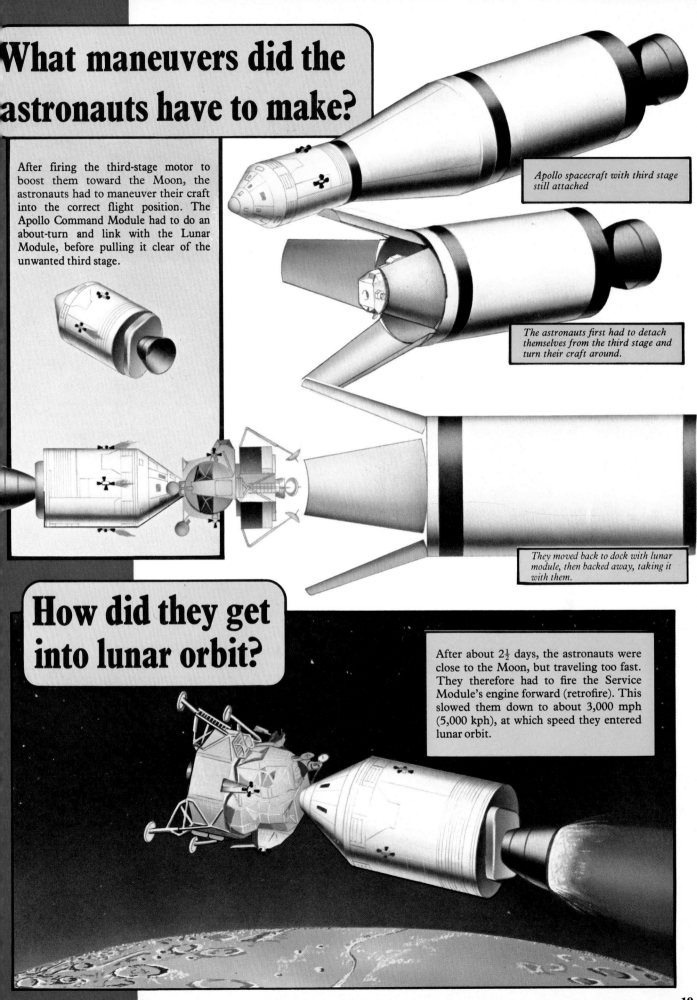

Apollo spacecraft with third stage still attached

The astronauts first had to detach themselves from the third stage and turn their craft around.

They moved back to dock with lunar module, then backed away, taking it with them.

How did they get into lunar orbit?

After about 2½ days, the astronauts were close to the Moon, but traveling too fast. They therefore had to fire the Service Module's engine forward (retrofire). This slowed them down to about 3,000 mph (5,000 kph), at which speed they entered lunar orbit.

How did the astronauts descend to the Moon?

Once in lunar orbit two of the three astronauts climbed into the Lunar Module (LM), in which they would descend to the Moon's surface. Having checked all its systems, they separated from the main craft. They fired the LM's engine to slow it down so that it dropped from orbit, and headed for the surface.

How did they land?

The astronauts also had to fire the LM's engine as a brake so that it could land softly on the surface. There was no other way of slowing it down. Parachutes could not be used, of course, because there is no air on the Moon.

Did they "fly" the Lunar Module?

The astronauts descended to within about 2,000 feet of the surface under computer control. Then they took over control of their craft so that they could select the best landing site, where there were no rocks or craters.

What did the Lunar Module look like on the Moon?

The Lunar Module was a strange-looking contraption, but it worked well. The springy legs cushioned the landing, and the foot pads stopped them from sinking too far into the lunar soil. Much of the body was covered with shiny gold foil to protect it from the Sun's heat.

Where did the landings take place?

Six lunar landings took place in the Apollo Project. The sites are marked on this map:

Apollo 11—Sea of Tranquility
Apollo 12—Ocean of Storms
Apollo 14—Fra Mauro crater
Apollo 15—Sea of Rains
Apollo 16—Cayley Plains
Apollo 17—Sea of Serenity

Who first walked on the Moon?

Astronaut Neil Armstrong was the first man to set foot on the Moon, on July 21, 1969. He was born in Wapakoneta, Ohio, in 1930, and became an aeronautical engineer and later a test pilot.

What did he say?

As Neil Armstrong stepped down onto the Moon's dusty surface, hundreds of millions of TV viewers back on Earth waited for his first words: "That's one small step for a man, one giant leap for mankind."

Was it difficult to walk on the Moon?

Because of the Moon's low gravity (about one-sixth of the Earth's), the astronauts at first found it difficult to move around. They soon found that it was best to move in a kind of loping stride, somewhat like a kangaroo.

THE MOONWALKERS In July, 1969, American astronauts achieved the goal President Kennedy had set in 1961—they set foot on the Moon. Between then and December, 1972, six pairs of astronauts—maybe we should call them "lunarnauts"—roamed the lunar surface for a total of 166 hours and covered nearly 60 miles (about 100 km). A new era had begun in the history of humankind.

Who was his partner?

Second man on the Moon was Edwin "Buzz" Aldrin, who was born in Montclair, New Jersey, also in 1930. On the Moon he was snapped in this famous photograph by Armstrong, who is seen reflected in his visor.

What did the Earth look like from the Moon?

The Apollo astronauts took thousands of stunning color photographs of the Moon. Some showed their home planet, the Earth. The Earth looked beautiful—swirls of white clouds could clearly be seen against the blue of the sea and sky, and the brown of the continents.

Did the men on the Moon have any vehicles?

The first two teams of astronauts explored the Moon on foot. The Apollo 14 astronauts used a cart to carry equipment. The last three teams had the use of a "lunar buggy" which allowed them to roam several miles away from their lander.

Footprints on the Moon

The footprints left behind in the soft lunar soil by the 12 astronauts who landed will be preserved for centuries in the weatherless environment.

What kinds of things did the astronauts do on the Moon?

LUNARNAUTS AT WORK The Apollo astronauts had a heavy workload to get through during their relatively brief stay on the Moon. But for months beforehand they had been practicing the techniques they had to use. Considering how cumbersome their spacesuits were, they performed their tasks very efficiently, with few mishaps. And they turned out to be excellent photographers.

One of the first things the astronauts did was to take rock and soil samples from their landing site, just in case they had to leave quickly. Then they explored their surroundings, photographing and describing anything interesting. Their other main task was to set up experiments.

What experiments did they set up?

They set up experiments to measure such things as waves through the lunar crust ("moonquakes"), the heat the Moon gives out, the presence of atomic particles, and magnetism. The instruments they left behind continued to send information for years afterwards.

What did they bring back?

The Apollo astronauts brought back a total of no less than 850 lbs (385 kg) of Moon rock and soil samples from the six different landing sites. The rock, from both highland and mare (sea) regions, has still not all been investigated thoroughly.

HOMEWARD BOUND The journey home from the Moon was just as hazardous as the journey out. The two moonwalkers had to return to the main spacecraft, which had to follow a precise flight path back. To hit the Earth's atmosphere at the wrong angle would have caused them to bounce off it or burn up in it. Either would have meant certain death.

How did the astronauts get off the Moon?

After their exciting and exhausting explorations of the Moon, the astronauts had to rejoin their colleague, who had been circling above them in the main part of the Apollo spacecraft. They blasted off from the Moon in the upper part of the lander, using the lower half as a launch pad.

How did they return to Earth?

The moment of launch was timed so that the lander would meet the main craft circling above. Then the astronauts maneuvered into position so that they could dock (link up) with the main craft. They then transferred to it, and sent the empty lander back to crash on the Moon. After final checks on the main craft's systems, the astronauts fired its rocket motor to boost it away from the Moon and into a flight path that would take it back to Earth.

Rendezvous and docking with main craft

Discard of lunar module

Lift-off from Moon

Firing of motors for homeward journey

Unlucky Thirteenth

The third Moon mission—Apollo 13—was truly unlucky, and the astronauts were fortunate to return alive. About 200,000 miles (300,000 km) from Earth an explosion occurred in the Service Module. They had to use the power and oxygen of the lander to survive.

How fast did they re-enter the Earth's atmosphere?

By the time the Apollo astronauts reached the Earth on their return journey, they were traveling at a speed of nearly 25,000 mph (40,000 kph)—or 7 miles (11 km) every second! They separated their Command Module from the Service Module, and plunged into the outer atmosphere—heat shield blazing.

How did they land?

The atmosphere acted like a brake and quickly slowed the Command Module down. Then parachutes opened above the craft to slow it down further. All of the Apollo landings were at sea, and recovery vessels were close at hand to remove the astronauts as quickly as possible.

What are Moon rocks like?

Microscopic cross-section of Moon rock

The Moon rocks can broadly be divided into two types. One is dark and very similar to basalt on Earth. The other consists of a mixture of rock chips cemented together, somewhat like breccia on Earth.

AFTER APOLLO The whole Apollo project is estimated to have cost more than $25 billion. But the scientific benefits from the Moon trips have been enormous. And the project accelerated the growth of new technologies, such as micro-electronics, which led to the introduction of pocket calculators. Many of the Moon's mysteries, however, remain, so we will continue to investigate this barren, lifeless world.

What have they told us?

The Moon rocks are very different in composition from Earth rocks. This indicates that the Moon almost certainly did not come from the Earth. The mare (sea) samples are much younger than those from the highlands, which are thought to be part of the Moon's original crust. The maria were probably formed when huge meteorites crashed into the crust and caused it to remelt.

Are spacecraft still visiting the Moon?

The United States is not at present sending spacecraft to the Moon, but the Russians are. These craft, called Luna, are robot craft designed to soft-land on the lunar surface. They are equipped with a movable arm with a drill at the end for boring into the surface.

What is special about them?

The drill bores into the surface and extracts a sample of soil. The arm delivers this into a capsule on top of the spacecraft. The upper part of the craft then takes off and returns the capsule to Earth.

What else has been landed on the Moon?

The most ingenious device the Russians have sent to the Moon is the robot vehicle called Lunokhod. The first one landed on the Moon in November, 1970. Lunokhod is driven by electric motors. The electricity comes from solar cells in its "lid." It is guided by scientists back on Earth, who "see" through its twin television cameras.

MOON BASE It is only a question of time before humans return to the Moon to set up a permanent base. Because of its airless skies, the Moon would make an ideal site for a deep space observatory, for example. Its first inhabitants will be scientists and engineers, but it will soon expand into a flourishing colony.

How will the first Moon base be built?

The first Moon base will be a simple construction. Probably it will be put together from the empty casings of the rockets used to propel the construction engineers to the Moon. The casings will be fitted out with extra equipment for their new role.

How will permanent bases be constructed?

A permanent Moon base will be built mainly underground, using tunneling machines "imported" from Earth. Under the ground, the Moon colonists will be protected from the scorching heat of the lunar day and the deathly cold of the lunar night.

Will they be self-supporting?

For a while, the Moon base will depend on Earth for all of its materials—oxygen, water, food, and equipment. But soon the colonists will begin to help support themselves. They will start growing their own food in vast greenhouses. They will recycle their water and wastes. They will begin mining their own raw materials for building and making metals. And they will set up chains of solar power stations to give them electricity.

Why will a Moon base be a good space port?

When journeys to other planets and space cities become common, the Moon will act as a major space port—for refueling operations and transfer of passengers and cargo. Because of its low gravity, spaceships would be able to come and go more easily than they could on Earth.

U.S. Manned Spaceflights (to the end of Project Apollo)

Mission	Crew	Date	Duration (hours)	Remarks
Mercury 3	Shepard	May 5, 1961	0.25	Suborbital flight–first American in space. (Spacecraft call sign Freedom 7)
Mercury 4	Grissom	July 21, 1961	0.25	Also suborbital; successful flight but spacecraft sank, astronaut rescued. (Liberty Bell 7)
Mercury 6	Glenn	Feb. 20, 1962	4.9	Three-orbit flight; first American in orbit; retropack retained when erroneous signal indicated heat shield possibly loose; capsule landed 37 miles (60 km) uprange. (Friendship 7)
Mercury 7	Carpenter	May 24, 1962	4.9	Also three-orbit mission; yaw error at manual retrofire caused 250-mile (400-km) landing overshoot. (Aurora 7)
Mercury 8	Schirra	Oct. 3, 1962	9.2	Six-orbit flight; capsule landed 4 miles (6 km) from recovery ship. (Sigma 7)
Mercury 9	Cooper	May 15–16, 1963	34.3	Twenty-two orbits to evaluate effects on humans of one day in space. (Faith 7)
Gemini 3	Grissom, Young	March 23, 1965	4.9	Three-orbit demonstration of the new spacecraft; maneuver over Texas on first pass changed orbital path of a manned spacecraft for first time; landed about 50 miles (80 km) uprange. (Molly Brown, only Gemini named)
Gemini 4	McDivitt, White	June 3–7, 1965	97.9	Four-day flight with White first American to walk in space, in 20-minute extravehicular activity (EVA); after 62 revolutions of Earth, landed 50 miles (80 km) uprange.
Gemini 5	Cooper, Conrad	Aug. 21–29, 1965	190.9	First use of fuel cells for electric power; evaluated guidance and navigation system for future rendezvous missions; incorrect navigation co-ordinates from ground control resulted in landing 87 miles (140 km) short; 120 revolutions.
Gemini 7	Borman, Lovell	Dec. 4–18, 1965	330.6	Longest Gemini flight; provided rendezvous target for Gemini 6; crew flew portions of mission in shirtsleeves for first time; 206 revolutions.
Gemini 6	Schirra, Stafford	Dec. 15–16, 1965	25.8	Rescheduled to rendezvous with Gemini 7 after original target Agena unmanned spacecraft failed to orbit; 6 launch postponed 3 days when launch vehicle engines automatically shut down 1.2 seconds after ignition; completed first space rendezvous; 16 revolutions.
Gemini 8	Armstrong, Scott	March 16, 1966	10.7	First docking of one space vehicle with another; about 27 minutes after docking, Gemini-Agena combination began to yaw and roll at increasing rates; mission was terminated midway through 7th revolution.
Gemini 9	Stafford, Cernan	June 3–6, 1966	72.4	Rescheduled to rendezvous and dock with augmented target docking adapter after original target Agena failed to orbit; docking proved impossible but three different types of rendezvous were completed; Cernan carried out more than 2 hours EVA; 44 revolutions.

Mission	Crew	Date	Duration (hours)	Remarks
Gemini 10	Young, Collins	July 18–21, 1966	70.8	First use of Agena target vehicle's propulsion systems; spacecraft also rendezvoused with Gemini 8 target vehicle; Collins had 49 minutes EVA standing in hatch, 39-minute EVA to retrieve experiment from Agena 8; 43 revolutions.
Gemini 11	Conrad, Gordon	Sept. 12–15, 1966	71.3	Gemini record altitude (739 miles; 1,190 km) reached using Agena propulsion system after first-revolution rendezvous and docking, Gordon fastened Agena-anchored tether to Gemini docking bar, and spacecraft later made two revolutions of Earth in tethered configuration; Gordon 33-minute EVA and 2-hour plus standup EVA; 44 revolutions.
Gemini 12	Lovell, Aldrin	Nov. 11–15, 1966	94.6	Final Gemini flight; Aldrin logged Gemini record total of 5½ hours extravehicular activity; 59 revolutions.
Apollo 7	Schirra, Eisele, Cunningham	Oct. 11–22, 1968	260.2	First manned flight of Apollo spacecraft Command and Service Module only; 163 revolutions. Like the subsequent Apollo spacecraft, it splashed down within 9 miles (15 km) of predicted landing point.
Apollo 8	Borman, Lovell, Anders	Dec. 21–27, 1968	147.0	First flight to the Moon (CSM only); views of lunar surface televised to Earth; 10 revolutions of the Moon.
Apollo 9	McDivitt, Scott, Schweickart	March 3–13, 1969	241.0	First manned flight of Lunar Module (LM); spacecraft call signs for communications identification when undocked: CSM "Gumdrop" and LM "Spider"; Schweickart 37-minute EVA from LM; 151 revolutions of Earth.
Apollo 10	Stafford, Young, Cernan	May 18–26, 1969	192.1	First LM orbit of Moon; call signs "Charlie Brown" and "Snoopy"; 31 revolutions of Moon (4 revolutions by undocked LM).
Apollo 11	Armstrong, Collins, Aldrin	July 16–24, 1969	195.3	First lunar landing; call signs "Columbia" and "Eagle"; lunar stay time 21 hours, 36 minutes, 21 seconds; Armstrong and Aldrin EVA (hatch open to hatch close) 2 hours, 31 minutes, 40 seconds; lunar surface samples 49 lbs (22 kg); 30 revolutions of Moon.
Apollo 12	Conrad, Gordon, Bean	Nov. 14–24, 1969	244.6	"Yankee Clipper" and "Intrepid"; stay time 31.5 hours; Conrad and Bean EVAs 3.9 and 3.8 hours; lunar samples 74.7 lbs (33.9 kg) plus parts retrieved from nearby Surveyor 3 unmanned spacecraft; 45 revolutions of Moon.
Apollo 13	Lovell, Swigert, Haise	Apr. 11–17, 1970	142.9	"Odyssey" and "Aquarius"; mission aborted after Service Module oxygen tank ruptured; using LM's oxygen and power until just before re-entry, crew returned safely to Earth.
Apollo 14	Shepard, Roosa, Mitchell	Jan. 31–Feb. 9, 1971	216.0	"Kitty Hawk" and "Antares"; stay time 33.5 hours; Shepard and Mitchell EVAs 4.8 and 4.6 hours; samples 97 lbs (44 kg); 34 revolutions of Moon.
Apollo 15	Scott, Worden, Irwin	July 26–Aug. 7, 1971	295.2	"Endeavor" and "Falcon"; first use of lunar roving vehicle (Moon buggy); stay time 66.9 hours; Scott and Irwin EVAs 6.5, 7.2, and 4.8 hours; Worden trans-Earth EVA 38 minutes; samples 170 lbs (77 kg); 74 revolutions of Moon.
Apollo 16	Young, Mattingly, Duke	April 16–27, 1972	265.9	"Casper" and "Orion"; stay time 71 hours; Young and Duke EVAs 7.2, 7.4, and 5.7 hours; Mattingly trans-Earth EVA 1.4 hours; samples 214 lbs (97 kg); 64 revolutions of Moon.
Apollo 17	Cernan, Evans, Schmitt	Dec. 7–19, 1972	301.9	"America" and "Challenger"; stay time 75 hours; Cernan and Schmitt EVAs 7.2, 7.6, and 7.3 hours; Evans trans-Earth EVA 1 hour; samples 243 lbs (110 kg); 75 revs. of Moon.

Landing on Another World

There will never be moments like them again. A fragile metal contraption containing two Earthmen is gingerly descending to the surface of another world—the Moon. The date is July 20, 1969. The contraption is "Eagle," the Lunar Module of the Apollo 11 spacecraft. The astronauts are Neil Armstrong and Edwin Aldrin, from the United States. Back on Earth at the Mission Control Center in Houston, Texas, the time is just after 4 o'clock in the afternoon. The spokesman at Houston is "talking down" the Lunar Module with the astronauts, with occasional comments by Apollo Control.

As Eagle swooped closer and closer to the lunar surface, the tension became electrifying. Hundreds of millions of people, eavesdropping on the dialogue between Earth and Moon, held their breath. Was it to be triumph or disaster?

HOUSTON: Eagle, you're looking great, coming up 9 minutes.
CONTROL: We're now in the approach phase, looking good. Altitude 5,200 feet.
EAGLE: Manual auto attitude control is good.
CONTROL: Altitude 4,200.
HOUSTON: You're go for landing.
EAGLE: Roger, understand. Go for landing. 3,000 feet.
EAGLE: 12 alarm. 1201.
HOUSTON: Roger, 1201 alarm.
EAGLE: We're go. Hang tight. We're go. 2,000 feet. 47 degrees.
HOUSTON: Eagle looking great. You're go.
CONTROL: Altitude 1,600 . . . 1,400 feet.
EAGLE: 35 degrees. 35 degrees. 750, coming down at 23. 700 feet, 21 down. 33 degrees. 600 feet, down at 19 . . . 540 feet . . . 400 . . . 350 down at 4. . . . We're

pegged on horizontal velocity. 300 feet, down $3\frac{1}{2}$ . . . a minute. Got the shadow out there . . . altitude-velocity lights. $3\frac{1}{2}$ down, 220 feet. 13 forward. 11 forward, coming down nicely . . . 75 feet, things looking good.
HOUSTON: 60 seconds.
EAGLE: Lights on. Down $2\frac{1}{2}$. Forward. Forward. Good. 40 feet, down $2\frac{1}{2}$. Picking up some dust. 30 feet, $2\frac{1}{2}$ down. Faint shadow. 4 forward. Drifting to the right a little.
HOUSTON: 30 seconds.
EAGLE: Drifting right. Contact light. Okay, engine stop.
HOUSTON: We copy you down, Eagle.
EAGLE: Houston, Tranquility Base here. The Eagle has landed.
HOUSTON: Roger, Tranquility, we copy you on the ground. You got a bunch of guys about to turn blue. We're breathing again. Thanks a lot.

HERE MEN FROM THE PLANET EARTH
FIRST SET FOOT UPON THE MOON
JULY 1969, A. D.

WE CAME IN PEACE FOR ALL MANKIND

NEIL A. ARMSTRONG
ASTRONAUT

MICHAEL COLLINS
ASTRONAUT

EDWIN E. ALDRIN, JR.
ASTRONAUT

RICHARD NIXON
PRESIDENT, UNITED STATES OF AMERICA

Index

A

Aldrin, Jr., Edwin E. ("Buzz"), 22, 34
Apollo, 11, 12, 28; astronauts, 14, 22, 24-25; experiments on Moon, 25; flights, 14, 18-27, 32-33; landing on Moon, 20-21; return to Earth, 26-27; rocket, 16; spacecraft, 14-15, 16, 18, 19, 20-21, 26
Archimedes (crater), 9
Armstrong, Neil A., 22, 34
atomic particles, 25

B

basalt, 28
bases, Moon, 30-31
Bergerac, Cyrano de, 7
Braun, Wernher von, 16
breccia, 28

C

calendar, 6
Cayley Plains, 21
Clouds, Sea of, 4
Collins, Michael, 34
craters, 4
Crises, Sea of, 4, 6

D

Diana (Moon goddess), 7
docking, 14, 26

E

"Eagle," 34
Earth, 5, 23
escape tower, 12, 18
escape velocity, 8, 9
experiments, 25
extravehicular activity (EVA), 32, 33

F

Fertility, Sea of, 4
Fra Mauro crater, 21
fuel, rocket, 17
fuel cells, 15

G

Gagarin, Yuri, 12
Gemini flights, 12, 13, 32-33
Glenn, John H., 12
gravity, 7, 8, 22

H

heat shield, 14, 17
highlands, 4, 25, 28
hydrogen, liquid, 17

K

Kennedy, John F., 12, 22
Kennedy Space Center, 17
kerosene, 17

L

launching tower, 12
literature, Moon in, 7
lunacy, 6
"lunar buggy," 23
lunar module (LM), 15, 19-21
"lunarnauts," 22, 24-25
Lunar Orbiter (U.S.), 11
Luna spacecraft, 9, 10, 11, 29
Lunokhod, 29

M

magnetism, 25
"man in Moon," 6
maria (seas), 4, 6, 25, 28
Mercury flights, 12, 32
meteorites, 28
micro-electronics, 28
Mission Control Center, 34
module, 13; command, 14, 19, 27; crew, 13; equipment, 13; lunar, 15, 19-21; service, 15, 27
Moisture, Sea of, 4
Moon bases, 30-31
"moonquakes," 25
myths about Moon, 6

N

Nectar, Sea of, 4

O

Ocean of Storms, 4, 21
orbit: lunar, 11, 19; parking, 18

orbital velocity, 8
oxygen, 27, 31; liquid, 17

P

Pacific Ocean, 5
parachutes, 10, 27
photographs, 5, 9, 23, 24
pocket calculators, 28
probes, soft-landing, 10, 11

R

Rains, Sea of, 21
Ranger probes, 9, 10
recovery vessels, 27
re-entry, 27
rendezvous, spacecraft, 13, 14, 26
retro-rockets, 10, 12
rocket motors, 10, 13, 15
rockets, 16-17
rocks: Earth, 28; Moon, 25, 28, 33

S

satellite, 8; artificial, 4, 8; natural, 4
Saturn V, 16-17, 18
science fiction, 7
Serenity, Sea of, 4, 21
Showers, Sea of, 4
soft-landing, 10, 11
solar cells, 9, 29
spacecraft, 5, 9; Apollo, 14-15, 16, 18, 19, 20-21, 26; Gemini, 13; Mercury, 12
space port, 31
spacesuits, 24
Sputnik I, 4
sub-orbital flight, 12
Surveyor probes, 11

T

Tranquility Base, 34
Tranquility, Sea of, 4, 21

V

V2 rocket, 16
Vapors, Sea of, 4
Vehicle Assembly Building, 17
Verne, Jules, 7

W

walking on Moon, 22
Wells, H. G., 7
"werewolves," 6

Lerner Publications Company
241 First Avenue North, Minneapolis, Minnesota 55401